JONATHAN I. ANGULO

How To
BECOME A
PHLEBOTOMIST
IN CALIFORNIA

FIND YOUR FUTURE SCHOOL
PREPARE FOR THE EXAM
TIPS FOR SUCCESS

Legal Notice

Disclaimer

All QR codes and websites are up to date and live as of June, 2023. If any of them are not working properly, please contact the author at *anguloauthor.com* for updated QR codes.

Copyright © 2023, **Jonathan I. Angulo**

ISBN: 979-8-9877323-0-4 (paperback)
ISBN: 979-8-9877323-1-1 (ebook)

First Printing, 2023

anguloauthor.com

How To
BECOME A
PHLEBOTOMIST
IN CALIFORNIA

FIND YOUR FUTURE SCHOOL
PREPARE FOR THE EXAM
TIPS FOR SUCCESS

Contents

HOW TO
BECOME A
PHLEBOTOMIST
IN CALIFORNIA

LEARN TO USE
A QR CODE

1 Open your camera and point your device at the QR code

2 Wait for camera to recognize and scan QR code

3 Click banner or notification when it appears on your screen

OKAY

4 Information associated with the QR code will automatically load

Note: Older phones might require that you download a QR scanner app first.

Introduction

Think of *How to Become a Phlebotomist in California* as a complete guide to your exciting new career path. It provides everything you need to navigate the journey of becoming a phlebotomist. If you want a professional career in healthcare, phlebotomy is an ideal place to start. The barriers to entry, such as education and certification, are relatively low compared to other healthcare career paths. The starting salary is good, and job opportunities are abundant. And with this job as your base, you can easily grow into other positions in the field.

Maybe you are fresh out of high school and looking for a profession that will get you into the medical field, help you pay for college while you work part-time, or help you decide if a career in healthcare is what you really want. Or maybe you are raising kids at home and want a jumpstart into a professional career with good pay and benefits. Or perhaps you are simply looking for a change in profession. Whatever the case, you probably have questions about what phlebotomy is like and where to start.

If you do, then you've found the right book to get answers to those and other questions.

As a licensed phlebotomist in the state of California since 2016, I know exactly how exciting yet stressful it can be venturing into a world where there is much at stake while knowing little about what to expect. You will need to navigate decisions about schooling, licensing, interning, and more, all while spending hundreds of dollars in the process. What you need is non-biased factual information from a reliable and experienced source. I am here to be that source for you.

I will hold your hand through the entire process. Chapter One helps you decide if this is really what you want to do. You will find valuable guidance on everything you need to know and do before you start school in Chapter Two. The following chapters help you wisely select your future school, prepare for your first day at school, and get the most out of your clinical internship. Following that, you'll learn all about applying for your certification exam and state license. The final chapter guides you in your search for your first job.

Although this book is mostly meant to guide people in the state of California, the information can be helpful regardless of which U.S. state you live in.

If you live outside California, the process is going to be basically the same, though of course you will need to clarify the certification and licensing guidelines for your area.

Let us turn the page and begin this new journey! Your new career awaits you!.

Chapter One

Why Become a Phlebotomist?

Phlebotomy is a very important and rewarding profession in the healthcare field. It is not for nothing that phlebotomists are often called the backbone of the hospital or laboratory.

Phlebotomists are healthcare professionals who assist in the running of laboratories mainly by collecting blood specimens. They help process most of the specimens collected as well as any that are brought to the laboratory, ensuring they are ready to be tested right away or to be sent to an outside laboratory. Their most valuable skill is the ability to collect blood samples from patients of all ages. Believe it or not, it is because of this valuable and perfected-over-time skill that even nurses and doctors go looking for phlebotomists to help them with difficult draws. (Fun fact: we call patients a "difficult draw" if it is not so easy to draw their blood right away, and they require multiple attempts; there are many reasons why this might happen.)

However, phlebotomists also help with collecting and handling other samples, such as sputum, urine, and stool. More recently, they have also stepped up to the call and provided enormous help in the collection of swabs for Covid testing and even given vaccines.

There are five main reasons why you might want to become a phlebotomist:

1. Accessible New Career
Training to become a phlebotomist is a relatively easy way to become a healthcare professional and join the medical field. It takes only 80–100 hours of training to become eligible to apply for licensure in California. It is also not too expensive— you can easily complete your schooling for less than $2,000. Compare that with other entry-level careers, such as becoming a medical assistant, for example. They go to go school for about nine months to a year and can spend more than $10,000. The lower cost and shorter training period do not only provide an easier road to launching your career. They are also a lower price to pay to find out if working in the medical field is what you want to pursue after all. I don't know about you, but in my own case, my wallet would be much happier if I found out that the medical field is not for me before committing to longer and more expensive training.

2. Opportunity to Work at a Job that Matters
Collecting blood and other specimens is of utmost importance in the care of a patient. The most common procedure you will become proficient at will be collecting blood samples via what is called a venipuncture, or the puncture of a vein. With the samples you draw, doctors are able to determine if a patient needs a new medication or if

their current medication is helping the way it is expected to. They can find out if someone has a disease and what they can do to treat it, they can find out if someone needs a blood transfusion, and many other things. The phlebotomist is the lynchpin to all that information.

3. Multiple Job Locations

Remember the day you had blood drawn at your doctor's office? Or the time you went to a laboratory (such as Quest Diagnostics, LabCorp, or ABC laboratories, to name a few) to have blood drawn? How about the time you or a family member were at a hospital, and someone came to your bedside to collect blood? It is highly likely that the person who collected the sample was a phlebotomist. That is one of the perks of being a phlebotomist—there are lots of places at which you could be hired. Here are some common work places and job titles.

Work Places
Doctor's Offices
Private Laboratories
Urgent Cares
Hospitals
Mobile Phlebotomists
Blood Donation Centers
Dialysis Centers
Covid-19 Collection Sites

Job Titles
Phlebotomist
CPT-1
Laboratory Technician
Lab Assistant
Travel Phlebotomist
Specimen Processor

Different work places might give their employees different job titles and different responsibilities, but becoming a phlebotomist opens the door for you to be hired at all these places and perform a variety of duties specific to each work place.

4. Good Pay for the Level of Experience

So, what is the pay like? Well, it depends on your experience, the type of place where you are hired, whether you are a full-time or part-time employee, and perhaps your ability to negotiate your pay rate. As of May 2021, according to the U.S. Bureau of Labor Statistics, California is the state with both the highest annual mean wage, at $48,070, and highest hourly mean wage, at $23.11. Not too bad, right? Of course, nothing is set in stone, and you could find yourself making more than that in no time.

5. Growing Job Market

On another good note from the U.S. Bureau of Labor Statistics, California is the state with the highest employment level for phlebotomists. Also, the employment rate for phlebotomists at the national level is projected to grow 22 percent between 2020 and 2030, a rate that is significantly higher than the average of 8 percent for all other occupations. This is great news for a future phlebotomist! You are going to be joining a profession that is projected to grow significantly in the coming years. That means more job openings and more opportunities for you to succeed.

In the next chapter, you'll find some often overlooked but important tips to address before you begin your phlebotomy classes.

Chapter Two

Before You Start School

As you probably know, there are some boxes that need to be checked before you can be accepted into a phlebotomy school. Some of them are mandatory requirements, and others I highly suggest because they will help you down the road. Let's take a look.

Common Prerequisites for Enrollment

Schools require prerequisites because they help ensure that the student can perform as necessary during the training. Other prerequisites are required because they will be needed as part of national certification or state licensure, or because a hospital, doctor's office, or laboratory requires them in order to ensure the safety of the patients and students. Here are some common prerequisites that might be required of you before enrolling in school:

- Medical terminology course

- CPR certification for healthcare providers
- High school diploma, GED, or endorsed/notarized foreign transcripts
- Background check
- Medical clearance from a qualified provider such as a doctor
- Proof of vaccinations, most commonly: Varicella, Hepatitis B, Tuberculosis, MMR, Tdap, Influenza, and Covid-19

This list is not all inclusive, and it might vary from school to school. I suggest that you ask the school about its requirements ahead of time, because not meeting them might delay you from enrolling in school or going into your clinical internship. It is also a good idea to meet all the prerequisites listed above even if they're not required by your school, because in the near future your upcoming employer will likely ask you for them regardless. It never hurts to be a step ahead of the game.

The prerequisites that might take you a little longer to complete are getting the medical clearance and your vaccinations updated. Delays might happen if it takes a long time to get an appointment with your doctor or your insurance needs to approve the vaccinations, which can take days or weeks to happen. Some schools will give you a form to take to your doctor's office for them to confirm that you are up to date on the vaccinations required. In order for the doctor's office to do that, you will most likely need an appointment and bloodwork done to make sure you do not need a booster of any vaccines.

If you do need a booster, the doctor's office might have to request an authorization from your insurance.

One of the more common prerequisites is a CPR certification for healthcare providers. Two well-known organizations that provide these certifications are the Red Cross and the American Heart Association (AHA), the latter being the most widely recognized and accepted by workplaces and schools. This certification can be obtained by completing an instructor-led course often called a BLS Provider course (BLS stands for basic life support). The course is about four hours long, costs about $50, and will teach you the basics of providing life support to a person in need, such as performing chest compressions on a patient whose heart has stopped beating or providing rescue breaths to a patient who has stopped breathing.

You can find an authorized training center to get your BLS Provider certification by visiting the AHA website. Here's a **QR code** that will direct you to the website where you can locate a training center near you.

The Language of Medicine

As you probably know, the healthcare field has its own language. Doctors, nurses, psychologists, medical assistants, and even medical billers need to be familiar with the language of medicine in order to coordinate care for patients and perform their job duties.

Medical terms—words used to describe a disease, body part, procedure, test, diagnosis, etc.—are almost always formed by two or more different prefixes, roots, and suffixes. For example, in the last chapter I talked about *venipuncture*. That word is created by the prefix veni-, which means vein, and -puncture, which means to pierce with. Therefore, *venipucture* means to pierce a vein, which is what we phlebotomists do when drawing blood. You will quickly become familiar with many medical terms like this just by breaking apart the individual parts of the term.

As a future phlebotomist and member of the healthcare field, you are going to need to learn this language sooner than later. But don't get scared or discouraged about this vital requirement. You won't need to be able to speak and understand another language right off the bat. Many people do not master the language of medicine in their entire careers; instead, they learn only what is needed to perform their job duties. But you can be a step ahead of your peers by taking a medical terminology course before you enroll or begin your phlebotomy classes. As a matter of fact, some schools require it.

Even if your school does not require it, taking a medical terminology course has some important benefits.

You are about to immerse yourself in a world that you may know little or nothing about. A phlebotomy class is usually fast paced and will teach you a lot of things. And while your school might teach you the basics of medical terminology, they are most likely not going to hold back on continuing their curriculum just because you're having difficulty learning about medical terms. If you're not understanding some of the things they are talking about, how are you supposed to learn more advanced concepts? You are most likely going to feel frustrated. Make things easier on yourself by learning that language ahead of time.

Let me share a little bit about my own experience on this particular topic. Before I began my phlebotomy training, I had the opportunity to take a free medical terminology course at my local community college, and I am so thankful that I did. It really helped me understand a lot of things that were talked about during class. I was not overwhelmed by learning medical terms, but only had to focus on the actual new phlebotomy material. I also felt confident about being able to pronounce those new terms without making a fool of myself. Some of those medical terms are long and complicated. Seriously! Try to say *cephalic vein, or basilic vein, or neuropathy, or even worse, otorhinolaryngologist.*

Fortunately for you, you do not need to look for a course, for I have come across a FREE medical terminology course online that I have taken myself and recommended to many others. It is offered by Des Moines University. While it is free, there is a $99 fee for a certificate of completion, which you'll need if your future phlebotomy school requires a medical terminology course in order to enroll. If you do not need the certificate, you can take the course as many times as you like for free. Free! Do I need to say more?

Here is a **QR code** to the course, or you can do a search for "Des Moines University Medical Terminology Course."

Liability Insurance

It is time we talk about legalities. If you live in California, which I suppose you do, then you probably know by now that we live in a state full of hungry lawyers. They are like sharks waiting for an opportunity to get a bite from anyone, and unfortunately, people in the healthcare business are most of the time . . . an easy prey!

While I do not wish to scare you in any way or form, let's be honest here. You are about to be trained how to invade someone else's body by puncturing it with a needle. As a student, you are allowed to make mistakes, and believe me, you will make them. We learn from our mistakes—that is what makes us grow professionally.

Unfortunately, some people are just looking for a mistake from someone to get an edge on them. There are way too many reasons I could list why someone might want to make a claim against you, many of which are out of your control. It could be that a patient did not like the way you treated them. Perhaps they asked you out on a date and, since you politely declined, they are claiming you abused them as retribution. Some people are just something else.

There are also more valid reasons someone might make a legal claim against you. Maybe you made a mistake when drawing their blood and ended up injuring them in a way that left them with long-lasting side effects, and they are claiming that you were negligent or committed malpractice. Negligent means that you failed to provide the level of care that someone with your level of training is expected to provide to others, usually due to an honest mistake. Malpractice means that you were aware of the possible consequences before making the mistake that led to an injury.

Let me give you a couple examples of cases in which having liability insurance might save you some money, as well as a possible headache:

- Defendant Expense Benefit and Deposition Representation: Imagine you are getting sued for whatever reason, and you need to appear along with your attorney to provide your testimony and answer some questions. Having liability insurance can reimburse you for the loss of your work wages while taking time off to appear at the deposition. It will also help you pay for your attorney.

- **Assault Coverage**: Imagine a patient or someone else injures you while at your clinical internship or at work. Having a liability insurance can provide you reimbursement for the expenses you might face in case you need medical care.

As you can see, having liability insurance can prove very helpful both during school and for the rest of your professional career. You can protect yourself against any legal claims among other things by simply purchasing a liability insurance policy. I highly recommend you do so. Some schools even require you to purchase one. In my experience, after attending different schools in the medical field, most schools recommend the same insurance provider. It is called HPSO, and they offer an insurance policy for students for as little as a single payment of $27, which will cover you during your entire time in school. They also offer discounts to recent graduates if you decide to maintain your coverage after school, which is not a bad idea considering their yearly coverage is for $3 million. Please, do yourself a favor and get coverage. You never know.

Here is the **QR code** to the HPSO website.

In the next chapter we will talk about how to find the best phlebotomy school for you.

Chapter Three

Choose the Best Phlebotomy School for You

Finding the right phlebotomy school is the single most important thing you will do while embarking on this journey. Your future school will hold the key to your success. They will train you not only to pass their course and the national certification, but they will also give you what you need to be successful while treating patients and meeting the expectations of your future jobs. Choosing the wrong school could cost you hundreds if not thousands of dollars more than you would otherwise have to pay. For example, if a school is not approved by the state, then you cannot get your license, so you will need to enroll in another school that is actually approved by the state—and that is time and money wasted. We will talk about this shortly. So, how exactly do know which school to choose?

Approved by the State

The first thing you have to make sure of is that the school is approved by the state of California to teach a phlebotomy course. Anybody can open a school and start teaching, but unless they are legit, they will not have an approval from the state. Now, just like a carton of milk, approvals do expire, so make sure to find out when their approval expires. At the end of this chapter, I will post a QR code to the state website where you can see a list of approved schools. There, you will also find an email address you can use to contact the state. I encourage you to reach out to them and ask them about the approval status of the particular school you are interested in.

Approved by a National Organization

Next, go to the school's official website and find out if that school program will allow you to sit for a national certification examination. There are many different certifying organizations out there, so again, make sure that the organization is one approved by the state. These organizations are independent from the school and the state. They serve as a bridge between the two to certify that students are knowledgeable enough to practice phlebotomy safely. We will discuss more about these national organizations in a later chapter. For now, reach out to the organization and make sure that the school is approved by them, and that their approval is current.

You will also want to check with the school regarding the passing rate of their past students when taking the national examination.

You do not want to go to a school that has a 50 percent passing rate, right? Ask them for recent statistics. Who cares if their passing rate was 95 percent five years ago? Without that national certification, you cannot obtain your license, so this is very important.

Think of it this way, you will pay hundreds of dollars to a school to train you and give you a certificate of completion. Any school can do that for you, but will their training be good enough for you to pass the national certification on your first attempt? That is what you really need—to be taught everything you need to get certified. Although you can certainly retake the test if you fail it, you want to make sure that you select a school that has a high first- time pass rate. Passing the test on your first attempt will save you money, time, and stress, and will put you on the path to getting your license faster.

Inquire About Clinical Internship

The next step is to ask the school about their process for sending students to do clinical hours. Clinical hours are when you practice your new skills in a real-life medical setting on real patients under the supervision of an experienced phlebotomist. Find out if the school will send you to a doctor's office, a hospital, or a laboratory. Also, ask them how long it usually takes for you to begin your clinical hours after you finish the classroom part of your training. You don't want to have to wait three months to begin your clinicals, right? That will only set you back on your track to complete your training.

Having to wait months to practice what you just learned can make the process harder, because knowledge will fade over time if not used. Also, one of the state requirements for getting your license is to complete a minimum of 40 hours of clinical practice during your training, so this is vital not only for personal growth, but also to satisfy the state requirement to apply for your license.

Look at reviews from other students
Find out what other students are saying about the school. Search the internet for reviews, or go to the school during teaching hours and ask the current students themselves what they have to say. Nothing better than hearing reviews on a firsthand basis.

What kind of information are you looking for? Find out if the school prepared them appropriately to pass the test on their first attempt. Inquire as to how proficient the teachers were at their job and if they made themselves available to answer questions outside of classroom time, such as responding to emails in a timely way. Find out if the school adequately follows up with their recent graduates and answers any questions they might have regarding the licensing process. Find out if they provided them with their diploma in a reasonable timeframe. You do not want to go to a school that will shut the door on you as soon as you graduate and will not provide any guidance or release the paperwork you need to get your license as soon as possible.

Some schools will even guide you in applying for the state licensure, and some will recommend their top students to local employers or help students look for a job. These are highly recommendable benefits that a school might offer. Imagine being the top of your class and having your school refer you to a local employer for a job opening. Being referred directly for a job position or simply being informed about a nearby job opening is a great deal that could help you land a job sooner.

Pick the Right Class Schedule

Lastly, there is a more personal decision that you might need to make. Some schools offer enrollment on a regular or an accelerated course. A regular course might have you commit to school two to three times a week for about two hours each. On the other hand, if you take an accelerated course, which is usually offered on the weekends, you might only have to be at school once a week for about eight hours. Here is where you need to weigh different factors when making this decision. For example, do you plan to be working a job while you go to school? If so, then probably it will be easier for you to look for a nighttime school or a weekend class, which can better accommodate your schedule. Likewise, if you have children at home, it is probably easier and cheaper to get a babysitter once a week rather than a few times a week; perhaps you should consider a weekend class too. On the other hand, perhaps it has been a few years since you last went to school, and you are a little unsure about going back to class. If that is the case, enrolling in an eight-hour class might prove very challenging to you, as a lot of new information will be thrown at you. It might be a better idea to enroll in a regular class that will meet a few days a week and give you some additional time to digest the new information during the week. Make sure to consider these factors when choosing your school, and don't be afraid to ask the school for their advice.

It is a lot of work finding the right school, isn't it? Absolutely! You are about to spend close to $2,000 dollars in the program—the least you can do is to make sure you are getting your money's worth. You will need your school to work for you, to help you succeed in their program and your clinical internship, and to guide you in applying for (and passing!) the national organization certification.

After all of the work I have asked you to do to find the right school, you will probably want to know which school I went to, and how things worked out for me. I went to school back in 2015, and I went through all of the steps described in this chapter. I am thankful for making the right decision and selecting a school that is rapidly expanding across the country: Phlebotomy Training Specialists. They were the best! They had everything I needed. I had to work in order to pay for the program, and they had a course that was offered on Saturdays that allowed me to do that and study during the week. They also had a payment plan that allowed me to pay in installments. Some schools will ask their students to purchase a third-party book, but luckily this school had their own book, and they gave it to us. That saved me some money in my pocket.

Once I finished the classroom part of the training, I had to wait for one or two weeks before they found me a place to do my clinical internship.

I was sent to a small privately owned laboratory; I learned a lot from that place, and I liked going there. I was fortunate enough to give a great impression there, and the supervisor called me about four or five months later and offered me a job at the laboratory. Lucky me! As for the national certification, the school guided me through the process of applying for certification, showed me what to study, and helped me prepare for the test. With all that help, I passed the test on the first attempt. The school also did some guiding as to how to apply for the state license. Overall, I got what I paid for and regret nothing.

As you can see, doing your research and picking the right school can either set you up for success or become a nightmare for you. I encourage you to do your due diligence and make an informed decision.

I know how to keep a promise, so here is the **QR code** to the state web page that lists approved schools in California.

Chapter Four

Your First Day at School

So, you have made all the right choices about your future school, you have made sure to meet any prerequisites, and you are now getting ready for your first day at school. What can you expect on your first day?

I think I have repeated this phrase a couple of times by now, but again I need to use it—sorry. But the fact is, your first day experience will vary from school to school. Also, things might vary depending on whether you enrolled in an accelerated course, weekends-only course, or a more regular course. If you enrolled in an accelerated or weekend course, you can expect to sit in class for possibly eight hours a day and cover a lot of information in every session. If you enrolled in a slower course, then you will most likely be covering a few topics in every class.

In general, you can expect your first day to be informational as to what to expect during the future sessions. They will probably cover deadlines for homework, turning in documentation to be eligible to go out to clinicals, and other housekeeping items.

In terms of actual teaching topics, you can expect to be taught about safety and ethical aspects of the profession, such as HIPAA, which is a major privacy law that every healthcare worker knows about. It stands for Health Insurance Portability and Accountability Act. You might also be taught during your first day about anatomy and the circulatory system. This is particularly important because you must know the human body, otherwise how could you expect to know where to draw blood from? Or how to select which vein to use? Not everyone's anatomy is the same, by the way. For some patients you will need to use your knowledge of anatomy, and other times only experience will allow you to make a wise decision.

If you are in an eight-hour class session, believe it or not, it is highly likely that you will have hands-on training on your first day of class, and you will begin drawing blood. This will definitely be a fun day. Your nerves will most likely go through the roof, but believe me you will be all right. Your future teachers will be there to guide you, so make sure to ask them questions. They want you to succeed. Depending on your school, you might begin drawing fake blood on some mannequins or go directly into drawing blood from your own classmates. Of course, any blood collected will be appropriately discarded and not tested, as it is just for practice.

Be aware that you are most likely going to be a volunteer at some point during class and let your fellow classmates learn by drawing your blood. Although you might be worried about letting inexperienced people draw your blood, I encourage you to be open minded about it. After all, you will be doing the same thing to your classmates and future patients during your clinical internship. It is wise to be on both sides of the situation and feel what the patient might feel when getting their blood drawn. This helps make us empathetic toward our patients.

Now, here's an interesting fact that may apply to you: some students find out during their first hands-on training that phlebotomy might not be the career of choice for them. The reason they find this out is because they faint at the sight of blood. Now, to be clear, fainting at the sight of blood is not a sign of weakness; it happens to a lot of people, and curiously enough, it is proven that men faint more often than women. Most times you cannot help it, and it will continue to occur. As a phlebotomist, you will learn how to deal with patients who suffer from these episodes of overreaction of their bodies, called *a vasovagal episode or vasovagal syncope*, as you draw their blood. It might be scary to witness that happening to a person, but you will soon learn that there are ways it can be prevented.

Unfortunately, if you are the person who suffers from these episodes, that might completely stop you from continuing with your training. If that happens to you, the school is most likely going to ask you to go see your doctor to be medically cleared to continue at school. But don't be scared about this happening to you because the odds are very low. In fact, I think I can count with my fingers how many patients I have had faint in front of me while drawing their blood during my nearly 10 years in the medical field.

Before you leave school on your first day, I advise you to ask your teacher for any tips or advice they might have for you to be successful in class. Also, ask them for any study handouts they might have that could help you better understand what they explained in class or provide a glimpse of what will be covered on the next class. For example, maybe they talked about HIPAA or anatomy on your first day, but it was covered lightly and you want to dig a little deeper to get a better understanding. If you ask your teacher, they might have some additional information they can share with you, such as a paper handout or an email they can send. In fact, you should also ask your teacher for their email or another way of communicating with them because you might have questions after class. Some teachers are happy to go above and beyond to help their students succeed, even after hours. Take advantage of their willingness.

Aren't you excited for your first day of school? I bet you are! I commend you for embarking on this new career. Be confident in yourself, study a lot, and be open to being taught lots of things.

Chapter Five

Your Clinical Internship

The clinical internship is the last part of your training, when you get to go out there and get your hands dirty—as well as your brain full of more knowledge and experience. This chapter not only gives you an overview of what your clinical internship will be like, it also provides advice on how to get the most out of it.

As soon as you are notified about your clinical internship site, make sure to ask your school for any documentation or requirements that the site is asking from you. That way you can begin gathering them and do not risk being pushed back from beginning your clinical internship until you meet them. For example, if you are being sent to do your clinical internship at a hospital, you are almost 100 percent for sure going to be asked to have a CPR certification, a medical clearance, and proof of vaccinations. If, however, you are going to go to a doctor's office, you might not need all of those things.

Give a Good First Impression

Regardless of where you are going to do your clinical internship, be it a hospital, a doctor's office, or a laboratory, you must go ready to learn a lot, do whatever you are asked by the person supervising you, and be in a mindset that you are there to learn and make mistakes. The first day of your clinicals, you can expect to be introduced to your supervisor, which will most likely be a phlebotomist, and you might also be briefed on the site policies and procedures.

Be prepared to give them any documentation that was requested from you, such as a CPR card or any paperwork required from your school. But most importantly, be sure to have your skills competency form with you. This form (formally called California Statement of Phlebotomy Practical Training) will be provided by your school, and you will eventually need to submit it to the national organization and the state. You will need to have completed at least 50 venipunctures and 10 skin punctures in order to graduate and become licensed, and this is the legal form where those tasks are documented. You will take it with you to your clinicals every single day. At the end of your clinicals, your supervisor will sign it, attesting that you in fact performed all of those punctures. Be sure to accurately record them, as you cannot graduate and get licensed without meeting those requirements.

On your first day, don't get discouraged if you are not allowed to draw any blood. Some supervisors want you to get familiar with their procedures first before allowing you to get in direct contact with the patients.

You might be able to improve your chances of drawing blood sooner if you show up motivated and portray yourself in the best possible light. For example, you will show great enthusiasm and willingness to help if you are volunteering to assist with other duties such as spinning the blood, working with the urine or stool samples, bagging or transporting specimens, or any simple tasks that ease the workload of your supervisor. Those simple things show your commitment to help, learn, and be a part of the team. Remember, you will be sharing the next 40 work hours at least with your supervisor. If you show initiative, I assure you they will be willing to reciprocate by helping you achieve your goals faster as well as teaching you everything they know. If a supervisor sees that you are not there just to do your hours and be done, but that you are there to help, learn, and improve, they will see your potential and might be more willing to give you their best advice, teach you the tricks they have learned, answer any doubts you might have, and help you achieve your goals.

It's important to know that most of the time, the person supervising you is not getting any extra payment for teaching you. They are doing it because they want to help future generations. Nevertheless, welcoming new students and teaching them can be a liability to them and the business. You could make a mistake that could make your supervisor look bad in front of their boss or the patients.

The supervisor is aware of this risk and is taking it because they want to help you. Therefore, it's in your interest to make yourself an asset and not a hindrance while you are there. Do not go in feeling entitled to do a lot of things on your first day. I have seen this happen many times.

You might be surprised what a little bit of kindness can do for you. Don't even get me started on how great you will look if you show up with a box of donuts on your first day. They will love you!

Some Clinical Advice

As the day to start your internship gets nearer, I can almost guarantee you will be worried about missing a vein while drawing blood. Try not to worry! Missing a vein is natural, and it will happen. You will get more confident and more proficient the more you practice. During your internship, you will be drawing blood from real patients, and people's veins come in different shapes and sizes. You might miss a vein because it is too deep or superficial and you misjudged how far to go with the needle. Maybe the patient moved the second they felt the needle or the vein may have "rolled." It could also be that your nervous, jittery hand failed and missed the mental target you had created for yourself. To be honest, that last reason will probably be the most common one in the beginning.

Regardless of the reason you missed the vein, you are probably going to feel really embarrassed and will want to withdraw the needle right away. If you feel a little more confident and have practiced enough, you might want to try and salvage the draw by doing some troubleshooting. If you do so and still are unsuccessful, it is time to tell your supervisor that you missed and let them take over, or just end the attempt there and withdraw the needle.

You might feel very disappointed after this. Just apologize to the patient and let your supervisor take over. It is highly likely at this point that the patient knows you are learning, either because you or your supervisor told them at the beginning or because the patient felt it. Yes, that's right, some patients are very clever and can tell a student a mile away. That can be a good thing, especially if they know that they are usually a difficult draw. They might tell you where other people usually draw them from, or they might even let you continue attempting to draw their blood in an effort to help you learn. On the other hand, some patients will request that you do not draw their blood because you are a student. Don't feel offended by this and just step back and learn nothing from this patient draw. You can still be around your supervisor as they prepare to draw the blood and feel for the vein they selected.

The more you get exposed to feeling different veins, the sooner you will become proficient at it. In fact, I suggest that you begin feeling other people's veins while you are at school, and try and feel the veins of your loved ones. The more practice, the better. You can even close your eyes or look away as you feel for them; this will help you train your fingers to feel for the vein instead of your eyes. This is particularly important since sometimes veins are too deep, and you can't see them.

Another important piece of advice for you: do not be afraid to ask questions. I know we want to look professional and well trained, and we want to show our supervisor that we know what we are doing, but remember that you are there to learn and are not expected to know it all.

Whenever the time comes that you are left solo to prepare your supplies and put the tubes in the right order before poking the patient, be sure to ask your supervisor any questions you have about the draw.

For example, you may have questions about the order of draw, or you may have doubts about a test, such as what test it is or which tube it goes in. Different laboratories have different requirements for their tests, and what you were taught in class might differ from how it's done where you are now. You do not want to draw the blood in the wrong order or in the wrong tubes, because this might be dangerous for the patient since the lab results might be compromised and delayed. Your supervisor might have to redraw that patient's blood. You can be proactive in becoming familiar with the tests and tubes by helping your supervisor gather the tubes they will need for the draw. Or, as you are spinning or putting the blood tubes in bags to be sent to the lab, you can check which tubes were drawn and then look at the doctor's order—that way you can try and find out on your own why the blood was drawn in those tubes.

Sell Yourself, Every Day!

Lastly, let's talk a little bit about networking during your clinicals. Networking means developing professional or social contacts with other people, and it is an important process that you need to engage in at some point in your life. As a new phlebotomist, networking is particularly important because it can make the difference between getting a job sooner rather than later.

A lot of times, jobs are made available first to people on the inside of job places or to people who are referred by a current employee. Why should you care about this? Because your clinical internship is a perfect opportunity to network and show yourself as a fit future employee at that place.

You'll look good if you do the basics such as showing up early, shaved, showered, and in uniform. Always be respectful and helpful to patients and staff. The staff there will certainly notice those things, and once you are done with your clinicals, it is highly likely that they will remember that helpful, timely, motivated student when an opening becomes available at that place. See what I'm getting at? You need to sell yourself every day you go to clinicals. It could pay off with a job offer from the site. A lot of students end up getting hired at the place where they do their clinical internship, so be ready to give them your daily best impression of yourself as a possible future employee.

In a nutshell, your clinical internship will be what you make of it. It will be very rewarding to finally put to practice what you have learned at school as well as to learn new things that will help you grow professionally. Be willing and ready to help with simple tasks, and give everyone a good impression. You got this! You have made it this far. I believe in you.

Chapter Six

Getting Your National Certification and License

In this chapter we will talk about how to become a licensed phlebotomist in California. Buckle up! This is going to be a long chapter with a lot of information to process.

How Phlebotomy Licensing Works in California

Things may vary significantly from state to state. Some states have more strict guidelines, and some states are more lenient. Fortunately for us in California, we live in a very stringent state that is not willing to make things super easy for us. In case you wondered, yes, that "fortunately" was sarcasm.

Almost any career in healthcare in California requires you to complete your training by an approved school.

Depending on the career, you might only have to get that diploma by completing school. For other careers, you might need to take a test from a national organization and receive a certification from them, or you might also need to apply to the state for licensure. Let me explain:

- A school diploma or a certificate of completion shows that you have successfully completed school.
- Getting a certification from a national organization shows that you have passed their national certification exam.
- Obtaining a license means that you have applied to the state and that you met their legal and training requirements needed to practice in your specific field.

For you to become a phlebotomist in California, you need to do all of the above. Some states, like Georgia for example, only require you to become nationally certified but don't require you to become licensed. Ohio does not even require a national certification—you only need to complete your school training to get a job.

Once you finish the final stretch of your journey to become a phlebotomist in California, you will be a licensed phlebotomist with a unique license number issued to you by the California Department of Public Health (CDPH). Doesn't that sound encouraging? Of course it does! Let us talk more about the entire process, shall we?

To be eligible to apply for licensure, you must first complete no less than 40 hours of classroom training and no less than 40 hours of clinical practice. Once you complete this training, you must then sit for a test from an approved national certifying organization. (Remember, your school should help you prepare to ace that test! They should also guide you during the entire process.) Once you pass that test, you will then become a certified phlebotomist across the nation. The organization that is certifying you will issue you a certificate that you will need to submit for your license application. Let us recap the steps so far:

1. Complete school training
2. Get nationally certified
3. Apply for state licensure

To apply for licensure to become a Certified Phlebotomy Technician I (CPT1), which is how California labels us, you will need other requirements during the online-only application process. I will mention some of them just so you are aware and can begin preparing accordingly:

- Email address
- Mail address
- SSN or ITIN
- Explanation of any felonies or misdemeanors
- High school diploma, GED, or endorsed or notarized foreign transcripts
- $100 application fee paid by credit or debit card
- Your certificates and forms scanned into a PDF file

The entire application process is not too complicated. The state of California even has some useful step-by-step videos of the entire application process, and at the end of chapter I will give you a **QR code** to one of those videos. Once your application is submitted, you should get your license emailed within two to six weeks. The state used to mail your license in the recent past, but now they email it to you. Your license is just a PDF file with your license number on it. Once you get your license, you can begin applying to jobs because you are now allowed to work as a phlebotomist.

Something else that is worth mentioning at this point is that the state requires you to renew your license every two years. In order to do so, you will need to complete at least six hours of continuing education (CE) from a CE provider accredited by the state of California.

"What are you saying? I need to take more classes?"

That's right! If you thought you were done with schooling after finishing your training, you were dead wrong! Things change often in the medical field; therefore, we need to keep ourselves up- to-date with current best practices and continue to enrich ourselves with more knowledge for the best of our patients.

Easing Into the National Certification
As you undoubtedly realized by now, becoming nationally certified is kind of big deal, and you will have to deal with it sooner than later. So, let's talk about those certifying organizations and how to always be on good terms with them.

Certifying organizations are for-profit companies that are not owned by the state but work with the state. Once you are in the process of finding your future school, you will realize that almost all schools are contracted exclusively with one organization. One school might certify their students through A organization, while another school works with B organization. While there might be some differences between the organizations, all of them are doing the same thing in the end. They are certifying that you, after successfully passing their examination, know the basic knowledge required by a phlebotomist to successfully perform the job duties according to national standards.

It would be a lot of work for the state to develop a standard test and do all of the logistics to ensure competency of all future phlebotomists. Instead, those certifying organizations do all of the dirty work for the state. If they can convince the state that they will do a great job ensuring that everyone that they will be certifying will be a competent and knowledgeable phlebotomist, the state will approve and work with that certifying organization. At the end of this chapter, I will post a QR code to the state of California website where you can see a list of approved organizations.

Interestingly, if a certifying organization is approved by many different states, that creates a benefit to us as phlebotomists. Imagine that you finish school and then some years down the line you move to another state, let's say Georgia. If you are a National Certified Phlebotomist, you were responsible enough to keep your certification current, and your certifying organization is one that Georgia has approved, you do not need to go to school again.

You can simply begin applying to jobs. Of course, other states might require you to obtain a license first, but still, with a current national certification you are just a few steps away from being able to job hunt.

Another good thing that a national certification can do for you is make you look better when applying for a job. Even though in California you must be nationally certified in order to obtain your license, once you have your license, you are no longer required to keep your national certification in order to apply to jobs or renew your license. Nevertheless, employers like to know that they are hiring a knowledgeable person for the job, a person who is committed to staying up-to-date with current practices. A national certification helps assure that.

Some people will let their certifications expire, and that shows how little commitment they have toward their profession. That is why an employer might decide to give an opportunity to someone with a national certification versus someone who just meets the minimum requirements of the state for continued licensing.

Let us talk about how your interaction with the certifying agency will most likely be.

At some point during your training process—it might be before, during, or after you finish your clinical internship—your school will tell you to create an online account with whatever organization they are contracted with, and then you will have to apply for your phlebotomy certification. The particular requirements to set up your online account might vary from organization to organization, but in general they all ask at the very least for:

- Email address
- First name (legal name)
- Last name (legal name)
- Residential address
- Phone number
- SSN

Two important things here. First, please make sure to spell your full legal name the way it shows up on your driver's license, school ID, state ID, or any other form of ID you have. The organization will have to verify that it is you taking the test and not someone else, so they might ask you to upload an ID to their website or bring with you one or two forms of ID the day of your examination. If the name does not match exactly how you entered it into their system, they might deny you to take the examination, and that would be a horrible thing to happen. Second, I don't know how confident you feel about disclosing your SSN to a non- government business, but in my own case, and in the case of some of my past classmates, we did not want to do it. What we did was call the organization and let them know that we did not feel confident disclosing our SSN to them for obvious reasons, and they provided us with a way around the application process without disclosing our SSN. Instead, they issued us an internal ID number that we entered on their system instead of our SSN. Again, your view on this issue might differ, so this is just a suggestion.

Once you create your online account, you will need to submit an application to become certified. If you have not yet finished school and do not have all the needed paperwork, you might need to have your school contact the organization to let them know that you are indeed one of their current students and that they should allow you to sit for the examination. However, if you already finished school, there are four main things that all organizations will ask you to submit either before or after you take the examination (but before they give you their certificate):

- High school diploma, GED, or endorsed or notarized foreign transcripts
- Copy of your phlebotomy technician diploma
- A clinical skills verification form
- Application fee (usually between $100–200)

Again, the requirements and the process might vary from organization to organization, and this list of things is not exhaustive, but it provides you with a general idea of what you can expect.

Preparing for the Examination

First of all, your time in the classroom will have prepared you very well to take this test. A lot of the material that you will be tested on will be in your textbook. Fortunately, there are also other ways to prepare yourself for the test.

Initially, I would suggest you ask your school for any study guides or any additional study materials that they might have. This is particularly important if you feel like you are performing weakly on a certain topic from class. In my experience, some schools have additional study materials they might provide to students who failed a quiz or test in order to help them study for the retake.

Next, go to the organization's website and see if they offer a study guide or practice test. I highly encourage you to purchase the practice test, which will likely cost between $20–40. Though it might seem pricey, this will give you valuable insight into what the questions will look like on the real test, and it will also test your knowledge—double win! Now, be aware that there are numerous third-party study tools out there, including books, websites, and phone applications. I have personally used some phone apps to help me prepare for other tests during my career, and although they can be super useful, make sure you do your due diligence when selecting them. If you decide to spend money on them, please make sure that they are meant to help you study for the test of the particular organization you are prepping for and that they are not too old, as things in the medical field are often changing. You do not want to buy a study book that was printed five years ago, right? Things might have changed a lot in that time.

On the day of the test, you will show up at your school or at a site designated by the organization. You will most likely be asked to leave all of your belongings at home or in your car and only bring with you one or two forms of ID. Expect to be treated like you just committed a crime and are being judged—these organizations treat testing very strictly!

You will most likely have to sit at the site for one to two hours, and it will be either a paper test or it might be a computer one. (The test format might depend on the organization's preferences or the capabilities of the site you are testing at.) Lastly, be ready to leave without knowing your results. The organization will either send you an email or upload the results to your online profile within a few days.

Recertification

The last thing I want to talk about is recertification. As I mentioned earlier, keeping your certification current shows your commitment to the profession, and it has benefits for you. Depending on your particular national organization, you might need to complete a certain number of CE hours (usually between 10–20) every year or two. You will also have to pay a fee to the organization to keep your certification. It is pretty close to the fee that you paid for the initial examination, but you do not need to sit for another test like you did before.

In my opinion, the best way to complete your CE is through the organization. Your organization will most likely offer several courses that you can take for free online. I encourage you to look for courses that are P.A.C.E. approved, and that the P.A.C.E. approval has not expired yet. P.A.C.E. stands for Professional Acknowledgment for Continuing Education. As I mentioned earlier in this chapter, the state of California requires you to complete six CE hours every two years to maintain your license regardless of whether you are going to keep your national certification active.

Your six CE hours must be P.A.C.E.-approved and non- expired, otherwise the state will not count them. Should your organization not offer those courses, a company called

Anderson Continuing Education has P.A.C.E approval, and it is likely that they will contact you by mail before you are due to renew your state license.

Like many things in life, letting your certification expire has its own consequences. If you let it expire for less than a year, usually organizations will just ask you to complete the CE and pay the recertification fee. However, if you let it expire for more years, they will ask you to complete more CE than usual, and they will also ask you to pay a higher fee to get it reinstated. After a certain number of years, the organization will not let you reinstate it anymore. Instead, you will have to retake the test. Imagine having to retake the test five years after graduation and having to learn almost everything all over again the way the books explained it, just like on your first day at school. Imagine having to study and memorize terms, definitions, and other concepts that are seldom used in real life once you finish school. You think it will be easy? Absolutely not! So don't let your certification expire.

Applying for Licensure

As I mentioned earlier, you will need to create an online profile at the CDPH website, and you will need to submit your application online. I recommend you do this as soon as possible while you are in school, but before you do so, you will need to get in contact with your high school and ask them to mail your certified transcripts to the state. Be aware that you might need to pay a fee for your transcripts to the school. Have them send the transcripts to the following address:

Laboratory Field Services - Phlebotomy Program

850 Marina Bay Parkway, Bldg. P 1st Floor
Richmond, CA 94804

High schools might take some time to process your request, so you want to start this process as soon as possible while you are in school to make sure you don't have to wait on them after you finish your phlebotomy program.

Once you have finished school and have in your hands the following documents, you are then ready to submit your application online for your licensure. Be sure to get them scanned into a PDF file.

- Certificate of completion of phlebotomy school
- National certification
- California statement of phlebotomy practical training

In order to successfully submit the application, you will also need the name and address of your high school, college (if applicable), phlebotomy school, and clinical site, as well as the dates in which you attended each of these. You will also need the name of your certifying organization, the certificate or ID number they provided you, and the effective day of your certification.

After successfully entering all of that information, you will be asked to upload the above-mentioned documents. Then, you have to attest that all of the information submitted is correct, sign, pay the fee online, and done!

You just need to wait for the state to do their job and send your new license.

As promised, here are a few QR codes to make your life a little easier. You're welcome!

List of approved certifying organizations in California.

Create your online profile at the CDPH website.

This is a QR code for a video created by the CDPH with step-by-step instructions on how to submit your application.

Chapter Seven

Finding Your First Job

Once you have finished school and are waiting for your license to arrive, it's time to begin searching for your first job as a phlebotomist. Job hunting will be your next full-time job, as it requires a lot of time doing research for job openings, creating your resume, and preparing for and attending interviews.

Where to Start

The best way to look for job openings is on the big websites that employers are using to post their openings, such as LinkedIn, Indeed, ZipRecruiter, and Glassdoor.

As I mentioned in Chapter One, there are many types of places where you can work as a phlebotomist, but it is also true that some places are more welcoming to new phlebotomists than others. Some places are a little more careful with hiring inexperienced phlebotomists due to the nature of the job or the patients that you might be exposed to (such as babies and children, which are more challenging when drawing their blood). I suggest you first look at blood donation centers, such as the Red Cross, because those places are well-known for welcoming and training new phlebotomists. Another job opportunity that is sometimes a good go-to for new phlebotomists is hospitals. The thing with hospitals is that most of the time their jobs are given to people who were referred there by an employee or to someone that already works or volunteers there.

In general, I don't recommend applying to private laboratories such as Quest and LabCorp until you have some job experience. Those places are usually highly sought after by other phlebotomists due to the job stability that they offer. While mobile phlebotomist sounds interesting and gives you some job flexibility, meaning you can choose when to work, you might also want to stay away from applying to those jobs at first. They usually require people who are more experienced with drawing blood from all ages and who know how to process special blood tests.

Stand Out From the Crowd

Is there anything you can do to increase your chances of getting hired? Absolutely! Probably the most important one is to get some volunteering experience first. Back in Chapter Five, I mentioned that you should try to be very helpful at your clinical internship site. Once you finish school, consider reaching out to that place again to see if they will allow you to volunteer a few days. Do that for a few weeks or months if possible, and that should really boost your chances. Employers like to see that you have some experience being a phlebotomist, even if it's only as a volunteer.

Reaching out to your school and asking them if they have any job leads is always to good thing to do as well. Also, if your goal is to work for a hospital, lots of hospitals have volunteer opportunities, so look into those and volunteer for them. That way you can begin learning how they work there, you can start selling yourself while you are there, and you can begin networking.

Other things you can do include completing the requirements that some jobs ask for, such as getting your BLS Provider certification. You can also complete courses such as a Blood Borne Pathogens course, which teaches you safety when coming into contact with blood and other body fluids (the AHA has an online course for about $22), and a medical terminology course (if you didn't do that before you started school). To some hiring managers, these few things show that you are more committed to being the best you can be, and that can potentially put you ahead of other applicants.

Prepare for Your Interview

Let us now change gears and start talking about that big day and what you can expect to happen. I'm talking about your interview day. The things you might be asked will vary according to the job position you're applying to and the type of facility. But in general, you can expect to be given some scenarios and asked what you would do in that particular case. For example, you might be asked how to handle drawing blood for the test "Lactic Acid." In this case, you should know that the blood should be collected without applying a tourniquet on the patient's arm and that you should cool the blood in ice immediately after collection. The exact same thing goes if you are asked to collect a sample for "Ammonia."

You could also be asked about the order of steps for collecting blood cultures. You might be given the scenario that a patient is diabetic and that you have failed to draw blood from the patient's arms. Is there any other place you could draw the blood from? Normally, you can try to draw blood from the patient's feet, but since the patient is diabetic, you need to get approval from the patient's doctor first. Expect to also be told that the doctor asked for certain tests followed by the question of what order you need to draw those samples. For example, let's say the doctor asked for a CBC, CMP, PT, and a blood culture. In this case you would draw blood for the blood culture first, then the PT, then the CMP, and lastly the CBC.

A more exciting and nerve-wracking possibility is that the person interviewing you will ask you to draw their blood. If that is the case, just stay calm and do as you were taught, and you will be fine.

Your Resume

A resume is a very important key to your success in applying for a job. It is the first thing, and unfortunately lots of times the only thing, that an employer will see about an applicant. A resume can get an employer to become interested in you, in giving you the benefit of the doubt, and inviting you to an interview. Or it can make an employer become uninterested and throw your application in the "not-a-chance" pile.

In my personal experience, a resume for people in the healthcare business has to be different from other styles of resumes. Our resumes do not need to contain our picture, extravagant font designs, or lots of colors. Leave that for people in jobs like graphic design or sales, where those things matter because they are tied to the job nature. In the healthcare business, especially when applying electronically and having a computer system pre-scan your resume for the right words, you need a concise, simple, and straight-to-the-point resume that clearly displays your qualifications and experience.

Should you need help writing your resume, I would suggest you take advantage of online courses out there that could give you valuable tips and insight. There are a lot of good choices that even offer videos and courses for free, such as YouTube or Udemy. Take advantage of those resources and use them to your benefit.

As we are nearing the end of the book, I do not want to miss the chance to thank you for taking the time to read this book and for getting ready to join the healthcare field and make of yourself a professional who is going to provide service to those in need.

The healthcare field is a fast-growing industry that will always have room for growth for those who want to pursue it.

For those of you who, like me, are always eager to learn new things and want to be able to help others as much as possible, you could certainly use the knowledge and experience gained from becoming a phlebotomist to help you transition into other professions. In my own case, shortly after becoming a phlebotomist, I realized that I wanted to learn more, so I enrolled in a course to become an EKG technician. Becoming an EKG technician opened some other doors for me and shined some light into another profession that I never thought of, which is how I became an EMT shortly after finishing my EKG technician certification. Recently, after years of being an EMT and saving for paramedic school, I became a paramedic in the middle of the Covid-19 pandemic. Paramedic school was definitely the most challenging, wearing, and mentally exhausting school I have ever ventured into, but it is very satisfying when you are able to help people at the worst times of their lives. This has been my greatest achievement so far, but I am not thinking of stopping there. There is something about gaining more knowledge that could help me in making the right decision when someone's life is at risk that I just cannot let go of. I need to pursue it.

With that being said, it is time you take the power of your own future in your hands and begin to make the right calls about what you really want to do. Do your research, study lots, be of benefit to society, and be safe out there.

About the Author

Jonathan I. Angulo became a licensed phlebotomist at the age of 20. From there, his passion for the medical field and for helping other people has led him to pursue other careers in healthcare, most recently becoming a paramedic during the Covid-19 pandemic. He has devoted his life to helping people in need and currently volunteers at a free clinic for low-income people at his local church by serving as a board member. When he is not at work, Jonathan enjoys walking, reading, and practicing archery. Jonathan currently works from home, as he, heartbreakingly, had to stop providing direct care to patients while battling cancer. He eagerly hopes to defeat his disease soon so he can go back to caring for patients and continue his education in pursuit of becoming a nurse practitioner.

Stay informed about upcoming books and learn more.

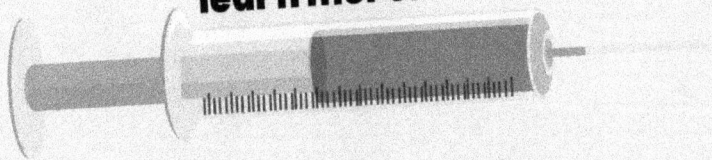

Coming Soon:

- **A day In The Life Of A Phlebotomist**
  -*Hospital Edition*

VISIT THE AUTHOR'S WEBSITE
anguloauthor.com

Sign up for announcements and discounts

Explore other books

Contact the author

EXPERIENCE WHAT A DAY IN THE LIFE OF A PHLEBOTOMIST IS LIKE

Follow the author as he performs his daily job duties at an outpatient laboratory. Go to anguloauthor.com to purchase.

Read on to look at Chapter One!

A DAY
IN THE LIFE OF A
PHLEBOTOMIST

Outpatient Laboratory *Edition*

Jonathan I. Angulo

Chapter One

A Bright New Day

As the clock turns to 7:00 a.m., I know it's time to get going. I zip up my hoodie and grab my lunch, all while trying not to make a lot of noise since my family is still asleep, and with that I am ready to leave my house. Leaving any later will not give me enough time should there be an accident or more traffic than usual on our already congested Los Angeles freeways. Fortunately, it is February and the days are starting to get bright earlier, and that usually makes traffic a little better in the mornings because drivers are able to see better.

As I make my way to the car, I'm hoping that I can get to work with some time to spare, especially since today is Monday, the busiest day of the week at the laboratory, and I'm the only phlebotomist there. I'm also the one who opens up the gates and lets the patients into the building. So, getting there late would probably mean getting the attitude of hungry patients who have been fasting—not consuming any food or liquids other than water—since last night. Some patients have been waiting outside in the cold for an hour or more because they want to be the first one I help out, just so they can get it over with and enjoy the rest of their day. That's why I always try to be there as early as possible—to avoid any more suffering for them, and for me as well.

I get in my car and begin driving, and soon enough I am joining the freeway in my old 2002 Mustang GT. I roll down the windows to get that morning chilly wind in my face—it always works wonders on Mondays to make me more alert as I drive half-asleep. The sight of a nicely flowing freeway makes me happy, because that means I will have enough time to stop by the McDonald's near my workplace and pick up a coffee to warm me up this cold morning and help me start the day.

McDonald's holds a very special place in my heart because it's where I worked to pay my tuition when I went to phlebotomy school last year. Although a lot of people complain about working there, I always saw the good of it. A steady job, lots of hours available, flexible schedule, and the opportunity to grow within the company. But what I miss the most is the conversations and relationships that I was able to build with some of my coworkers.

I still remember working a shift there as manager when I got a call from the supervisor at the laboratory. I had met the supervisor during my clinical internship at the lab when I was training to become a phlebotomist—a medical professional who draws blood and takes other samples from patients. The supervisor was at the laboratory almost daily because the place was about to change ownership and she had to help with the transitioning. I suppose me being a team player while I was learning there left a great impression on her, which was why she decided to call me for a job interview. The previous phlebotomist, who taught me during my internship, had moved away, and the supervisor thought I could be a good fit since I already knew how the business operated.

Sometimes it still feels surreal that I was able to get this job at such a young age. I still wonder if it was pure luck or my actual qualities. How could I, a 20-year-old, be running that place almost by myself? How did I transition so quickly from being an inexperienced student phlebotomist at this exact same place to being the only phlebotomist in charge of opening, closing, and helping patients of all ages?

While the answer is still unknown to me, I want to believe that it was a little bit of both luck and hard work that got me here. Regardless of the reason, I committed to work in healthcare in order to do good for people, and this job is allowing me to do just that.

After a 12-mile drive through the local freeways and streets, here I am at the McDonald's drive-thru at 7:40 a.m., about a mile from the lab, waiting to get my coffee. While I wait, I begin creating a mental checklist of the things I will have to do once I get to work and before opening the door for patients to come inside the lab. This way, I will already know what to do when I get there and will not waste any time.

As I am driving past the building before I park, the smell of coffee hanging in the air in my car, I get a glance at the people standing outside waiting for me to open the gates. Since the lab is inside a square-shaped single-floor building surrounded by other medical offices, all of the patients have to wait outside for me to open the gates and allow them inside, regardless of which office they are visiting. Today there are about 15 people standing outside already. Oh, god, it seems like it's going to be one of those busy Mondays. Good thing I had time to grab coffee, because I am going to need the caffeine boost. I park my car, take a deep breath, and here I go to help out patients to the best of my ability.

www.ingramcontent.com/pod-product-compliance
Lightning Source LLC
Chambersburg PA
CBHW060418050426
42449CB00009B/2022